The Story of
Folk Music

The Story of Folk Music

MELVIN BERGER

S. G. PHILLIPS *New York*

Library of Congress Cataloging in Publication Data
Berger, Melvin.
  The story of folk music.

  Bibliography: p. 121
  Includes index.
  SUMMARY: Examines the evolution of American folk music due to the influences of politics, different personalities, and musical instruments.
    1. Folk music—History and criticism.   [1. Folk music]
I. Title.
ML3545.B45   781.7'73   76-18159
ISBN 0-87599-215-3

    3   4   5   6   7   8   9   0

Contents

My life flows on in endless song
Above earth's lamentations,
I hear the real, though far-off hymn,
That hails a new creation.

No storm can shake my inmost calm,
While to that rock I'm clinging.
It sounds an echo in my soul.
How can I keep from singing?

—*White Spiritual*

CHAPTER ONE

This Is Folk Music

Four thousand people at a folk concert jump to their feet, cheering and clapping, as the singer finishes "Blowin' in the Wind." A college student sits alone with a guitar, quietly picking out the notes of a song he is composing.

Blacks and whites, with arms linked, march for civil rights, singing "We Shall Overcome." An eighty-

Thousands of people attend outdoor folk music concerts and festivals.

year-old woman in the mountains of Kentucky sings a song that she learned from her grandmother.

A group of teen-agers clap their hands and tap their feet as they loudly sing "When the Saints Come Marchin' In." A mother softly hums her baby to sleep with a lullaby written by a long-forgotten composer.

With deep emotion, the members of a small southern country church join their voices in "My Lord, What a Morning." Kids in New York City chant and sing as they skip rope and play other street games.

Young and old, black and white, rich and poor, trained musicians and those without lessons, in large groups and alone, and in every part of the country, more people than ever before are listening to, singing, and composing folk songs.

Folk music has always been a part of our American culture. During the Revolutionary War, American soldiers sang "Yankee Doodle" as they marched to battle. Settlers heading west to California in 1849 sang "Sweet Betsy from Pike." Deckhands on the big sailing ships chanted "Haul Away, Joe," while raising the foresail for their voyages to faraway lands.

Around 1900, Texas farmers laughed at their misery in "The Boll Weevil Song." Later, Oklahoma farmers told how their rich topsoil was blown away in the dust storms of the 1930s by singing "So Long, It's Been Good to Know You."

In Pennington County, South Dakota, a 1936 homesteader plays fiddle to pass the hours. (Photo by Rothstein, courtesy Library of Congress)

More recently, we showed our opposition to war and to killing by singing "Masters of War." And we sang "Big Muddy" to make clear our determination not to follow our leaders blindly and without questioning.

Most of us can recognize a folk song when we hear one. There is something special about a folk song that makes it different from other kinds of songs.

One of the special features of most folk music is that it was made up by people who were not trained composers. (Some folk music was written by trained composers, but more about that later.) Folk songs are created by people who have a story to tell, a love to express, or a joke they want to share. The songs come from slaves dreaming of freedom, from cowboys driving their cattle, and from prisoners working in chain gangs. Children playing games, farmers planting their fields, workers on the picket line—all of them are makers of folk songs.

These songs are passed along and spread by word of mouth, from person to person, and from town to town. The person who makes up a song sings it for his or her family, friends, and neighbors. Some of the people who hear the song like it enough to learn the words and tune. Each one sings it for his or her family, friends, and neighbors. On and on the folk song is passed, from place to place, from generation to generation. The same song often travels great distances and lasts for hundreds of years.

When a song spreads by singers learning it from other singers, it is said to be part of an oral tradition. It is different from the music of professional composers, which is spread by being published and recorded. The oral tradition is an important part of folk music.

As the music is passed on by the oral tradition, it goes through many changes. Imagine that you make up a song and sing it to three people. Each one learns the song and sings it. But the first person has a bad memory. Each time he sings the song, he puts in new words and notes to replace those he has forgotten. The second person finds the tune hard to sing. He changes some of the notes to make it easy for his voice. The third person thinks that the song is old-fashioned. He makes changes in the words so that they fit the times better.

The same sort of changes take place in real folk songs. As they are passed on, the singers forget, adapt, and modernize the songs. The words and music keep on changing in many different ways. This idea of continual change is another important part of folk music.

A good example of continual change in folk music is the song "Billy Boy." It probably began as a folk song in England about three hundred years ago. We believe that the original went something like this:

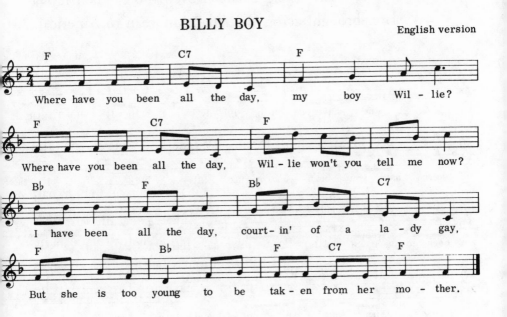

BILLY BOY

English version

Where have you been all the day, my boy Wil - lie?
Where have you been all the day, Wil - lie won't you tell me now?
I have been all the day, court - in' of a la - dy gay,
But she is too young to be tak - en from her mo - ther.

[11]

From England the song was taken to Ireland.
There it took on this form:

Irish versi

Where have you been all the day, Bil-ly Boy, Bil-ly Boy? Where ha

you been all the day, me Bil-ly Boy?_____ I've been

out with Nan-cy Gray, and she's sto-len me heart a-way,__ She's me

Nan-cy, tick-led me fan-cy, Oh, me char-min' Bil-ly Boy.

The same song changed even more when it was
later brought across the Atlantic Ocean to America:

American versi

Oh,__ where have you been, Bil-ly Boy, Bil-ly Boy? Oh,__

where have you been charm-ing Bil-ly?_____ I have

been to seek a wife, She's the dar-ling of my life, She's a

young thing who can-not leave her mo-ther.

[12]

Some changes improve the folk song. There is a general polishing and tightening up. The words become more direct and clearer. A text that originally had a limited, narrow meaning is broadened so that it has some meaning for everyone. The tragic song is given deeper emotion, the humorous song is made funnier.

The music, too, is improved. The melody becomes more natural and expressive. Changes in the rhythm add variety and interest to the music. The words and music fit together better.

There are some changes, though, that make the song worse. Sooner or later, these changes are dropped. So, over a long stretch of time, most folk songs get better and better.

Very few folk songs were made just to entertain. Most folk songs have a purpose or function. The purpose may be to help people to work, to dance, to play, or just to pass the time. It may be used to tell a story or to protest an injustice; to woo a lover, or express hatred for an enemy; to build up the singer's courage or to stir up the enthusiasm of others; to carry on the legends and history of a nation.

Most folk songs are meant to be sung, rather than played on instruments. Usually they are fairly short. Some are made long by repeating parts of the song over and over again. Often the melody and the words are quite simple. As a song is passed on, any unnecessary parts are dropped. Also, a song must be

[13]

rather simple for people to learn it and sing it for others.

The most popular type of folk music is the ballad. The word comes from the Italian *ballare*, "to dance." Originally it was a song that was sung between the sections of a dance. Now it is any song that tells a story, usually of just a single event, and quite often a tragic event. Most ballads are divided into stanzas of about four lines each, sometimes with a chorus that is repeated after each stanza.

Here is one of the best-known ballads:

BARBARA ALLEN

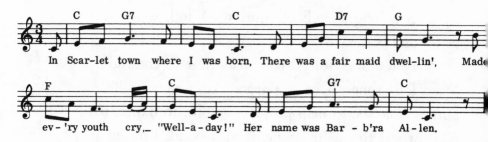

In Scar-let town where I was born, There was a fair maid dwel-lin', Made ev-'ry youth cry,— "Well-a-day!" Her name was Bar - b'ra Al - len.

In Scarlet town where I was born,
There was a fair maid dwellin',
Made ev'ry youth cry, "Well-a-day!"
Her name was Barb'ra Allen.

'Twas in the merry month of May,
The green buds they were swellin',
Sweet William on his death-bed lay,
For the love of Barb'ra Allen.

He sent his servant to her door,
To the place where she was dwellin',

[14]

"O Miss, O Miss, O come you quick,
If your name be Barb'ra Allen!"

So slowly, slowly she came up,
So slowly she came nigh him,
And all she said when there she came,
"Young man I think you're dying."

He turned his pale face toward the wall,
For death was in him dwellin',
"Goodbye, goodbye, my dear friends all,
Be kind to Barb'ra Allen."

As she was walking o'er the fields,
She heard the death bell knellin',
And ev'ry stroke did seem to say,
"Unworthy Barb'ra Allen."

Her eyes looked east, her eyes looked west,
She saw his pale corpse comin';
"O bearers, bearers, put him down,
That I may look upon him."

"O father, father, dig my grave,
Go dig it deep and narrow.
Sweet William died for me today;
I'll die for him tomorrow."

They buried her in the old churchyard,
Sweet William's grave was nigh her;
And from his heart grew a red, red rose,
And from her heart, a brier.

They grew and grew to the steeple-top
Till they could grow no higher;
And there they tied in a true-love knot,
The red rose and the brier.

Work songs were created to help men at their work. Some songs set a rhythm to help sailors haul up the anchor or to help railroad workers lift heavy lengths of track. Other songs tell of the heartsickness of the cowboys and sailors, away from their wives and sweethearts for months at a time.

A very well-liked work song is:

BLOW THE MAN DOWN

Oh, blow the man down, bul-lies, blow the man down, To me way, hey, blow the man down, Oh, blow the man down, bul-lies, blow him a-way, Give me some time to blow the man down!

Oh, blow the man down, bullies, blow the man down,
To me way, hey, blow the man down.
Oh, blow the man down, bullies, blow him away,
Give me some time to blow the man down!

As I was a-walkin' down Paradise Street,
To me way, hey, blow the man down,
A pretty young damsel I chanced for to meet.
Give me some time to blow the man down!

She hailed me with her flipper, I took her in tow,
To me way, hey, blow the man down,
Yard-arm to yard-arm away we did go.
Give me some time to blow the man down!

[16]

But soon as that packet was clear of the bar,
To me way, hey, blow the man down,
The mate knocked me down with the end of a spar.
Give me some time to blow the man down!

As soon as that packet was out on the sea,
To me way, hey, blow the man down,
'Twas devilish hard treatment of every degree.
Give me some time to blow the man down!

So I give you fair warning before we belay;
To me way, hey, blow the man down,
Don't never take heed of what pretty girls say.
Give me some time to blow the man down!

A number of folk songs originated as an accompaniment to dancing. Here the words are not too important, but the song must have a good, steady, clear beat. One of the most popular of these songs is "Skip to My Lou."

SKIP TO MY LOU

Lost my partner, what'll I do?
Lost my partner, what'll I do?
Lost my partner, what'll I do?
Skip to my Lou, my darling.

I'll get another one, prettier than you, [3x]
Skip to my Lou, my darling.

Gone again, skip to my Lou, [3x]
Skip to my Lou, my darling.

Flies in the buttermilk, shoo fly, shoo, [3x]
Skip to my Lou, my darling.

Little red wagon, painted blue, [3x]
Skip to my Lou, my darling.

Cat's in the cream jar, what'll I do? [3x]
Skip to my Lou, my darling.

Can't get a redbird, a blue bird'll do, [3x]
Skip to my Lou, my darling.

Kitten in the haystack, mew, mew, mew, [3x]
Skip to my Lou, my darling.

These are our verses, the rest must come from you, [3x]
Skip to my Lou, my darling.

Still another group of songs is made up of
nonsense and humorous songs. For out-and-out
silliness, American nonsense songs are outstanding.
From the tall stories of the lumberjacks to the
foolishness of the southern mountain folk, it is hard to
find better. A favorite funny song is:

ARKANSAS TRAVELER

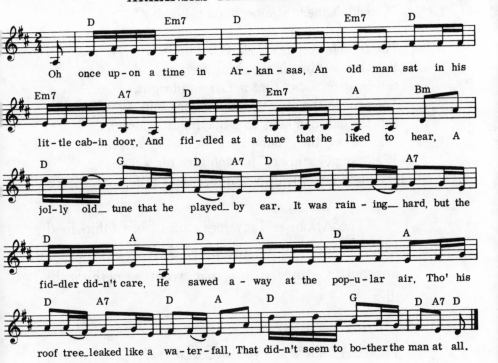

Oh once up-on a time in Ar-kan-sas, An old man sat in his lit-tle cab-in door, And fid-dled at a tune that he liked to hear, A jol-ly old tune that he played by ear. It was rain-ing hard, but the fid-dler did-n't care, He sawed a-way at the pop-u-lar air, Tho' his roof tree leaked like a wa-ter-fall, That did-n't seem to bo-ther the man at all.

O once upon a time in Arkansas,
An old man sat in his little cabin door,
And fiddled at a tune that he liked to hear,
A jolly old tune that he played by ear.
It was raining hard, but the fiddler didn't care,
He sawed away at the popular air,
Tho' his roof tree leaked like a waterfall,
That didn't seem to bother the man at all.

A traveler was riding by that day,
And stopped to hear him a-practicing away;
The cabin was afloat and his feet were wet,
But still the old man didn't seem to fret.
So the stranger said: "Now the way it seems to me,
You'd better mend your roof," said he.

[19]

But the old man said, as he played away:
"I couldn't mend it now, it's a rainy day."

The traveler replied: "That's all quite true,
But this, I think, is the thing for you to do;
Get busy on a day that is fair and bright,
Then patch the old roof till it's good and tight."
But the old man kept on a-playing at his reel,
And tapped the ground with his leathery heel:
"Get along," said he, "for you give me a pain;
My cabin never leaks when it doesn't rain."

"The Arkansas Traveler" came from Ohio in the 1850s. Before singing the song, there was usually an improvised conversation that went something like this:

Traveler: How do you do, stranger?

Old Man: I do as I please.

Traveler: Stranger, do you live here?

Old Man: I don't live anywhere else.

Traveler: Have you lived here all your life?

Old Man: Not yet.

Traveler: How did your potatoes turn out last year?

Old Man: They didn't turn out; we dug them out.

Traveler: Can I stay here all night?

Old Man: Yes, you can stay right where you are, out on the road.

Traveler: How far is it to the next tavern?

Old Man: I reckon it's upwards of some distance.

Traveler: How long will it take to get there?

Old Man: You'll not get there at all if you stay talking to me.

Traveler: Where does this road go?

Old Man: It don't go nowhere, it just stays put!

There are spirituals, both white and black. There are love songs, children's game songs, and lullabies. There are songs of protest, songs of prayer, songs of joy, and songs of despair. There are all of these and many, many more. And they are all folk songs.

Usually it is very clear whether or not a song is folk music. Nobody would call a Haydn symphony or a singing commercial a folk song. But what about songs like "Swanee River" and "O Susanna"? They are part of the oral tradition and are often sung as folk songs. Yet they were composed by a trained, professional composer, Stephen Foster.

And what about songs like "When the Saints Come Marchin' In" and "Greensleeves"? They are both folk songs. Yet they have been arranged, recorded, and performed so many times by professional musicians that we forget their folk-music origins.

In some ways these songs, and many others like them, are folk songs. In some ways they are not. But it is really not terribly important to put a label on every single song. It is much more important to sing, to hear, to learn more about, and to make up new folk songs.

Perhaps Big Bill Broonzy had the best answer when asked whether a particular song was a folk song. "It must be," he said. "I never heard a horse sing it!"

CHAPTER TWO

Folk Music — American Style

The modern American folk song is a tasty "dish" of many flavors. It should be. It is made up of the best ingredients, collected from countries all over the world.

Over the last four hundred years, many thousands of immigrants came to these shores. They brought with them folk songs and traditions, as well as performance styles, from their native lands. Each group made a special and unique contribution to the rich mixture of American folk music.

Since the British played such an important part in settling our country, it is not surprising that their music is a most important part of our folk music. The early colonists brought several hundred ballads and other kinds of folk songs over with them from England. Some of these songs are very old. They date back to the fifteenth and sixteenth centuries.

No one knows who wrote these songs. Most were probably made up by people with no formal musical background; some were surely written by professional composers. But since they have been passed along by

Several centuries ago, minstrels crisscrossed England, singing the news of the day as they traveled from town to town. (Illustration by Robert Galster).

oral tradition, and since they have folk-like melodies and words, they are accepted today as folk songs.

A good number of the old songs were made up by minstrels. These singers crisscrossed the country bringing the news of the day from town to town, from castle to castle, from tavern to tavern. They wrote songs that told of the floods in the south, of the birth of a baby boy to Lady Edith, of the battle between Prince Henry and Lord Philip, and so on. In the days before newspapers or radios, the minstrel songs helped tell people what was happening beyond their villages.

Many of the later British folk songs first appeared in print on large sheets of paper called broadsides. The broadsides were sold in the street by peddlers. Often the broadside ballads just had the words printed, with the name of the tune to which the words should be sung. Just as with the earlier minstrel songs, the broadside ballads told the news of the day for the large numbers of people who could not read.

Most English folk songs, you will find, are divided into stanzas. The chorus-verse form is one popular type of stanza song. The melody of the chorus and verse is repeated over and over again. The words of the verse, though, keep changing. They carry the story of the song. The words of the chorus stay the same; they are repeated after each verse.

In general, the words are the most important part of the English folk songs. The melody and rhythm are simple and less important. The songs themselves deal with many different subjects. Probably the greatest number are love stories—some true, some invented. Other popular subjects are war and battles, sea adventures, crime and criminals, and funny stories. And there are a good number about heroes who triumph over difficulties.

Most English folk songs are solo songs. They are performed without harmony or accompaniment. The performer sings with a hard, high-pitched, nasal voice quality. During the song, the singer keeps his or her body stiff, and shows no emotion or expression.

THE GOLDEN VANITY

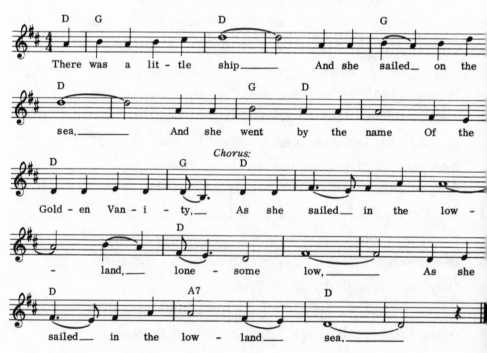

There was a little ship
And she sailed on the sea,
And she went by the name
Of the *Golden Vanity*,
   As she sailed in the lowland, lonesome low
   As she sailed in the lowland sea.

There was another ship
That sailed upon the sea,
And the name that they called her
Was the *Turkish Roveree*,
   As she sailed, *etc*.

"O Captain, Captain mine,
Now what will you give me,
If I sink, if I sink
That *Turkish Roveree?*"
   As she sailed, *etc*.

"O I will give you gold
And I will give you fee,
And my fairest daughter
Will be wed to thee,
   If you sink her," *etc*.

So he then bared his breast
And away swum he,
And he swum till he come
To the *Turkish Roveree*,
   As she sailed, *etc*.

He had a little tool
Just fitted for his use,
And he bored nine holes
And he bored them all at once,
   And he sank her, *etc*.

Then swiftly he swum back
To the cheering of the crew,
He swum till he come
To the *Golden Vanity,*
   As she sailed, *etc.*

"O Captain, Captain mine,
Won't you take me on board,
Won't you do unto me
As you said that you would do?
   For I'm drowning," *etc.*

He hoisted up his sails
And away sailed he,
And he left that poor sailorboy
To drown in the sea,
   To drown in the lowland, lonesome low,
   To drown in the lowland sea.

The first settlers from England made their homes along the Atlantic coast. They set up their farms on good land, and opened shops in towns. They lived near others, and were in close social, business, and musical contact with other people. Many of their old songs changed as they heard new songs and music from other countries.

By the time of the American Revolution, though, all of the good coastal farm land was taken. New settlers were forced to farm the hill country in the southern Appalachian Mountains. There were no roads in this area. Few people passed through. These later English settlers were isolated. Their songs have been preserved with only slight changes through the years. In fact, in the early twentieth century, the British folk-music scholar, Cecil Sharp, was able to find more examples of English folk songs in their original form in the Appalachian Mountains than he was able to find in England!

If you see one of the old English songs in print today, you may notice a "Child number." This number refers to a listing in a catalog of three hundred English ballads collected, organized, and classified by the American scholar, Francis James Child (1825-1896). Since there are so many versions of each song, the Child number is a good way for the singer to identify a particular song.

Emigrants from many countries came to America in search of a better life. At the same time, blacks from West Africa were brought to America against their will. Under slavery, the African folk music that they brought with them was forgotten. But their African musical traditions have had a tremendous impact on the developing American folk music.

The main purpose of many of the African songs was to retell the history of the people. The songs often fall into a leader-group, or call-response, pattern. One person sings a line or a section, and then the group answers.

The music features rhythm over words and melody, and usually has quite complicated rhythmic

The early slaves in America brought their music over from Africa. They often clapped their hands and tapped their feet; sometimes they used home-made drums to accompany their dancing and singing.

patterns. There is frequent use of syncopation, which is an accent at an unexpected time. African songs are divided into short, repeated sections. The words usually stay the same, while there are slight differences in the rhythm or melody. Though the patterns change, the basic beat, or tempo, does not.

The African style calls for a raspy, throaty singing voice. Good performers are expected to change voice qualities for different songs. They are also expected to improvise and make up slight changes in the music.

African music uses instruments. Percussion, wind, and stringed instruments are used in Africa to accompany the songs. Without their instruments, the

[30]

WHERE IS THE QUEEN?

Ghanaian Folk Song
Adapted by M. B.

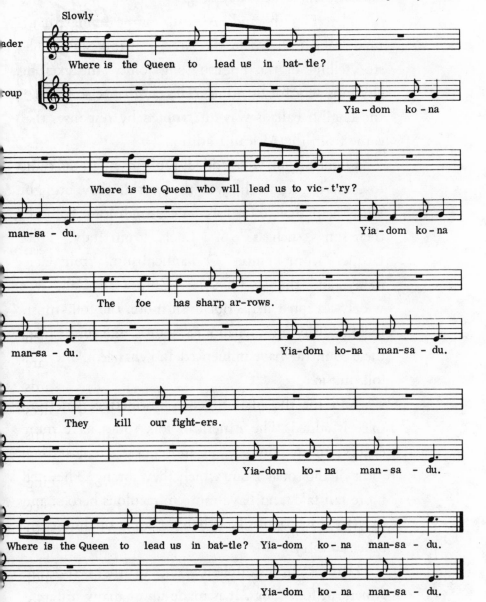

Slowly

ader — Where is the Queen to lead us in bat-tle?

roup — Yia-dom ko-na

Where is the Queen who will lead us to vic-t'ry?

man-sa - du. — Yia-dom ko-na

The foe has sharp ar-rows.

man-sa - du. — Yia-dom ko-na man-sa - du.

They kill our fight-ers.

Yia-dom ko-na man-sa - du.

Where is the Queen to lead us in bat-tle? Yia-dom ko-na man-sa - du.

Yia-dom ko-na man-sa - du.

black slaves in America clapped their hands and tapped their feet as they sang.

The English and African musical ingredients mixed and mingled in the American folk songs. The storytelling of the English song joined the exciting rhythms of African music. The chorus-verse form of the English ballads was interrupted by responses that came from the African tradition.

Other flavors were added, too. As emigrants came to America from all over the world, they brought with them their own folk-music traditions. Some of their songs, such as "Santa Lucia" from Italy, "Frère Jacques" from France, "O Tannenbaum" from Germany, and the Jewish song "Zum Gali Gali," are widely accepted here. But even more, the folk-music melodies, rhythms, harmonies, words, and forms from these countries have influenced and changed American folk music.

And for the final touch a distinctive American spice is added. The American folk songs have more energy, more humor, and more raw strength than most of the songs from which they sprang. They tell more tall tales and have more miraculous heroes, and they are downright sillier than the songs of almost any other country.

Here is an example of one of the best-loved American folk songs. It is made up of many different elements, shaped and formed into this unique creation.

[32]

THE ERIE CANAL

We were forty miles from Albany, forget it I never shall,
What a terrible storm we had one night on E-ri-e Canal.
   Oh, the E-ri-e was a-rising
   And the gin was a-getting low,
   And I hardly think we'll get a drink,
   Till we get to Buffalo, [2x]

We were loaded down with barley, we were all of us full
   of rye,
And the Captain he looked down on me with a doggone
   wicked eye.
   Oh, the Erie, *etc.*

Three days out from Albany a pirate we did spy,
The black flag with the skull and bones was wavin' up on
   high.
   Oh, the Erie, *etc.*

[33]

We signaled to the driver to hoist the flag of truce,
And we found it was the *Mary Jane* just out of Syracuse.
 Oh, the Erie, *etc.*

The cook, she was a grand old pal, she wore a ragged
 dress,
And we run her up upon the mast as a signal of distress.
 Oh, the Erie, *etc.*

We were three nights out of Hudson, when we struck a
 rock of coal;
It gave the boat an awful shock and stove in quite a hole.
 Oh, the Erie, *etc.*

We hollered to the Captain, on the towpath treadin' dirt;
He jumped on board and stopped the leak with his old
 red-flannel shirt.
 Oh, the Erie, *etc.*

The Captain, he got married; the cook, she went to jail;
And I'm the only sea-cook's son that's left to tell the tale.
 Oh, the Erie, *etc.*

CHAPTER THREE

The Politics of Folk Music

There is an old idea that singing people are happy people. Well, that is just not so. Some of the best and most moving folk songs grew out of people's misery and frustration. They are the moans of beaten slaves and the grunts of men at hard labor, the songs of prayer and songs of protest. As folk singer Woody Guthrie said, "Hard luck is one thing that you sing louder about than you do about boots and saddles, or moons on the river, or cigarettes a-shining in the dark."

It is very hard to silence a song of protest. Books can be burned, printing presses can be smashed, and people can be killed. But once a song has been sung, it cannot be stilled or stopped from being passed along.

Some of the best-known American songs of protest come from the struggles of the black slaves for freedom and equality. Many of the slave songs are

This old print shows slaves enjoying themselves as they sing
and dance to the music of a banjo player. Most of the slave
music, though, was not for fun. It was to help them with their
work or to express their dreams of freedom.

spirituals. They tell about such Bible figures as David,
Moses, Daniel, and Joshua. These heroes triumphed
over great odds and helped the Jewish people free
themselves from slavery. In the Negro spirituals these
same heroes are symbols of the slaves' struggles to gain
their freedom. "Little David" describes how an
enslaved people can overcome their masters to win
their freedom.

LITTLE DAVID

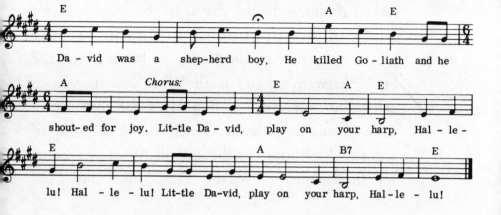

David was a shepherd boy,
He killed Goliath and he shouted for joy.
   Little David, play on your harp,
   Hallelu! Hallelu!
   Little David play on your harp,
   Hallelu!

Tell you what little David done,
Picked up a rock and out he run.
   Little David, *etc.*

Goliath swung his iron sword,
But David hit him with the power of God.
   Little David, *etc.*

Goliath was a mighty man,
But God put strength in David's hand.
   Little David, *etc.*

Watch the sun, how steady she run, .
Don't never let it catch you with your work undone.
   Little David, *etc.*

[37]

Many spirituals are about rivers. The river had several meanings to the slaves. In one sense it was a symbol of the barriers of slavery. To cross the river meant to be free. In another sense the river was the border between life and death. When you die, you go across the river. Then, to the slaves, the river sometimes meant the Atlantic Ocean. In 1822 a group of wealthy Americans bought land in Africa as a home for freed American slaves. They called this land

DEEP RIVER

Liberia. Crossing the river meant crossing the ocean to Liberia.

In the moving spiritual "Deep River," river has still another meaning. It was the name of a Quaker meeting house in North Carolina. Freed slaves were brought together there before being placed on ships that would take them to Liberia.

Only a few slaves, however, were able to return to Africa. Others escaped to the North, beyond the grasp of the slave owners. In "Follow the Drinkin' Gourd," the slaves were not only inspired to escape, but they were given specific directions on the route.

Pegleg Joe, a one-legged sailor, made several trips through the countryside north of Mobile, Alabama, teaching this song to any slaves who would listen. He left the marks of his left shoe and the round hole of his right peg leg on the ground or carved on trees. The directions were to head north in the spring to the Tombigbee River, to follow it to the Ohio River, and then on to safety. The Drinking Gourd, which you may know better as the Big Dipper, helps point the way north.

FOLLOW THE DRINKIN' GOURD

When the sun comes back, and the first quail calls,
Follow the drinkin' gourd,
The old man is a-waitin' to carry you to freedom,
Follow the drinkin' gourd.
    Follow the drinkin' gourd,
    Follow the drinkin' gourd,
    For the old man say,
    "Follow the drinkin' gourd."

[40]

Now the river ends between two hills,
Follow the drinkin' gourd,
There is another river that runs on other side,
Follow the drinkin' gourd.
   Follow the drinkin', *etc.*

Now that river bank makes a fine old road,
Follow the drinkin' gourd,
The dead trees show the way to go, left foot, peg foot,
   goin' on,
Follow the drinkin' gourd.
   Follow the drinkin', *etc.*

Where the little river meets the great big one,
Follow the drinkin' gourd,
There the sailor is a-waitin' for to carry you to freedom,
Follow the drinkin' gourd.
   Follow the drinkin', *etc.*

Freedom from slavery, when it finally came, did not mean an end to suffering for the blacks. Out of their bitter experiences after Reconstruction came a new song form, the blues. The blues were usually freely sung, with the singer adding extra words at the end of each line. A few notes, called blue notes, were purposely sung flat. The favorite subjects of the blues were disappointments in love and the search for a better way of life. "Alabama Bound," a blues folk song, dates back to the early 1900s.

ALABAMA BOUND

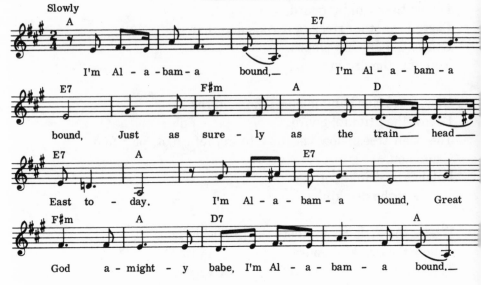

I'm Alabama bound, [2x]
Just as surely as the train head East today,
I'm Alabama bound,
Great God a-mighty babe,
I'm Alabama bound.

Why don't you be like me? [2x]
Drink your wine and soda, babe, but let the whiskey be,
But let the whiskey be,
Great God a-mighty babe,
But let the whiskey be.

I'm Alabama bound, [2x]
If the train don't run tonight, I got a mule to ride,
My home ain't here at all,
Great God a-mighty babe,
My home ain't here at all.

Oh, make me drunk again, [2x]
If you catch me getting sober, baby,
Oh, baby make me drunk,
Great God a-mighty babe,
You got to make me drunk.

Oh, don't you leave me here, [2x]
If you leave me, honey babe, just leave a dime for beer,
Just leave a dime for beer.
Great God a-mighty babe,
Just leave a dime for beer.

There was another whole set of songs to accompany the heavy work of black men. While wielding axes, picks, sledge hammers, or hoes, while carrying heavy logs or large bales of cotton, while laying long

Gang-labor songs accompanied the heavy work of black men as they did such jobs as lining up long lengths of railroad track. (Photo courtesy Library of Congress)

stretches of railroad track—these songs gave rhythm to their work, helped them pass the time, and released some of the anger they felt about their hard life.

One of the most familiar gang-labor songs is "The Hammer Song." Collectors have heard it sung in Virginia, Georgia, North and South Carolina. It is sung slowly, often with a grunt on the silent beat, the moment when the men swing their heavy axes or picks.

THE HAMMER SONG

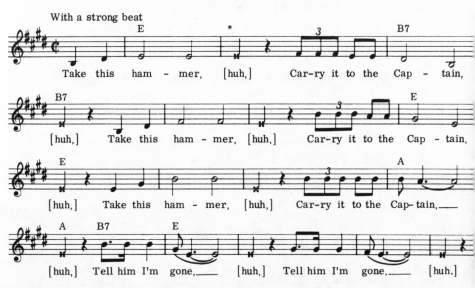

* Spoken, or even better, grunted.

Take this hammer, huh, Carry it to the Captain, huh, [3x]
Tell him I'm gone, huh. [2x]

If he asks you, huh, "Was I runnin'?" huh, [3x]
Tell him I'se flyin', huh. [2x]

If he asks you, huh, "Was I laughin'?" huh, [3x]
Tell him I'se cryin', huh. [2x]

I don't want no, huh, Corn bread 'n molasses, huh, [3x]
Hurts my pride, huh. [2x]

Repeat first verse

The white miners toiling in the coal pits of Kentucky and West Virginia had their songs, too. They worried about the many accidents and diseases that broke the miners' bodies, and brought them to an

THE HARD-WORKING MINER

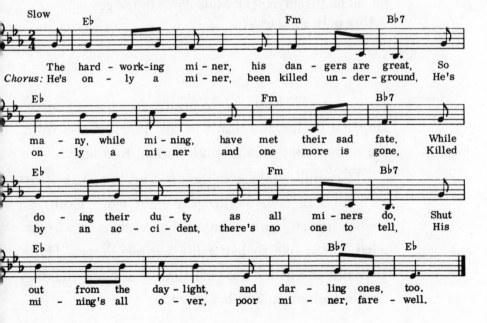

The hard-work-ing mi-ner, his dan-gers are great, So
Chorus: He's on-ly a mi-ner, been killed un-der-ground, He's

ma-ny, while mi-ning, have met their sad fate, While
on-ly a mi-ner and one more is gone, Killed

do-ing their du-ty as all mi-ners do, Shut
by an ac-ci-dent, there's no one to tell, His

out from the day-light, and dar-ling ones, too.
mi-ning's all o-ver, poor mi-ner, fare-well.

[45]

The hard-working miner, his dangers are great,
So many, while mining, have met their sad fate,
While doing their duty as all miners do,
Shut out from the daylight, and darling ones too.
   Chorus:
   He's only a miner, been killed underground,
   He's only a miner and one more is gone,
   Killed by an accident, there's no one to tell,
   His mining's all over, poor miner farewell.

He left his dear wife, and little ones, too,
To win them a living as all miners do;
But while he was working for those whom he loved,
He met a sad fate from a boulder above.
   He's only a miner, *etc.*

A miner is gone; we'll see him no more,
May God be with the miner wherever he may go.
God pity the miner, protect him as well,
Shield him from danger while down in the ground.
   He's only a miner, *etc.*

early grave. "The Hard-Working Miner," a simple, sad song on life and death in the mines, comes from the coal-mining area around Harlan, Kentucky.

The mill workers in South Carolina had their own kind of hell, working at giant cloth looms as long as sixteen hours a day. These workers also knew what it was like to live a life without hope. "Hard Times in the Mill" was first sung in a cloth-making mill in Columbia, South Carolina.

[46]

HARD TIMES IN THE MILL

Ev'ry morning at half-past four,
You hear the cooks hop on the floor.
   It's hard times in the mill, my love,
   Hard times in the mill.

Ev'ry morning just at five,
You gotta get up, dead or alive.
   It's hard times, *etc.*

Ev'ry morning right at six,
Don't that old bell make you sick?
   It's hard times, *etc.*

The pulley got hot, the belt jumped off,
Knocked Mr. Guyon's derby off.
   It's hard times, *etc.*

Old Pat Goble thinks he's a hon,
He puts me in mind of a rooster in the sun.
   It's hard times, *etc.*

[47]

Ev'ry night when I go home,
A piece of cornbread and an old jaw bone.
   It's hard times, *etc.*

Ain't it enough to break your heart,
Have to work all day, and at night it's dark.
   It's hard times, *etc.*

In time, the oppressed workers in various industries began to organize into labor unions. Songs were among the strongest weapons the union members had, both on the picket line and at union meetings.

Joe Hill was an early union song writer. He was executed in 1915 on a murder conviction. Many people believe it was a frame-up to silence this daring song writer. Joe Hill's most famous song is "Pie in the Sky." In this song he wrote new words to the old church hymn "Sweet Bye and Bye."

PIE IN THE SKY

Text by
Joe Hill

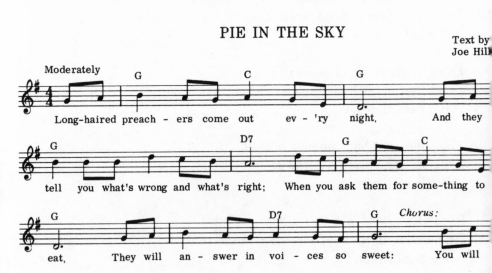

Moderately

Long-haired preach - ers come out ev - 'ry night, And they tell you what's wrong and what's right; When you ask them for some-thing to eat, They will an - swer in voi - ces so sweet: *Chorus:* You will

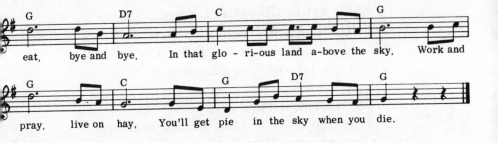

eat, bye and bye, In that glo - ri-ous land a-bove the sky, Work and
pray, live on hay, You'll get pie in the sky when you die.

Long-haired preachers come out ev'ry night,
And they tell you what's wrong and what's right;
When you ask them for something to eat,
They will answer in voices so sweet:
    Chorus:
    You will eat, bye and bye,
    In that glorious land above the sky.
    Work and pray, live on hay,
    You'll get pie in the sky when you die.

Oh, the Salvation Army they play,
And they sing and they clap and they pray,
Till they get all your coin on the drum,
Then they'll tell you when you're on the bum:
    You will eat, *etc.*

Holy Rollers and Jumpers come out,
And they holler, they jump and they shout:
"Give your money to Jesus," they say,
"He will cure all diseases today."
    You will eat, *etc.*

If you fight hard for children and wife,
Try to get something good in this life,
You're a sinner and a bad man, they tell;
When you die you sure will go to Hell.
    You will eat, *etc.*

[49]

Workingmen of all countries, unite!
Side by side we for freedom will fight.
When the world and its wealth we have gained,
To the grafter we'll sing this refrain:
Final Chorus:
You will eat, bye and bye,
When you've learned how to cook and to fry.
Chop some wood, 'twill do you good,
And you'll eat in the sweet bye and bye.

More recently, demonstrators and marchers made up new songs to help their struggle for freedom, justice, and civil liberties for all. There was a firm feeling of determination and solidarity among both the black and white protestors in this movement. One of their songs, "We Shall Not Be Moved," bound these people together. It gave them the strength and courage to face the angry mobs and armed police officers.

"We Shall Not Be Moved" actually started life as a spiritual in the early years of the nineteenth century. In the 1930s the Southern Tenant Farmers' Union used it to bolster the spirits of the union members as they struggled against the landowners. And now it is one of the most stirring songs of the civil rights movement.

WE SHALL NOT BE MOVED

We shall not, we shall not be moved, We shall not, we shall not be moved, Just like a tree that's plant-ed by the wa-ter, We shall not be moved.

We shall not, we shall not be moved,
We shall not, we shall not be moved,
Just like a tree that's planted by the water,
We shall not be moved.

Black and white together, we shall not be moved, [2x]
   Just like a tree, *etc.*

Stand and fight together, we shall not be moved, [2x]
   Just like a tree, *etc.*

The union is behind us, we shall not be moved, [2x]
   Just like a tree, *etc.*

Another old spiritual, "I'm Gonna Sit at the Welcome Table," was adapted in the 1960s as part of the same struggle. "Welcome table" in the old song referred to heaven or to a happier life on earth. To the thousands of blacks who sang the song at "sit-ins," where they asked for service in whites-only restaurants, the "welcome table" was a counter where blacks and whites could sit side by side.

[51]

WELCOME TABLE

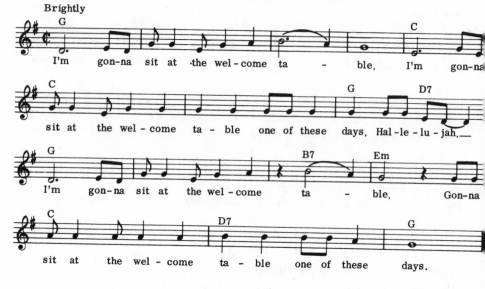

I'm gonna sit at the welcome table,
I'm gonna sit at the welcome table one of these days,
   hallelujah,
I'm gonna sit at the welcome table
Gonna sit at the welcome table one of these days.

I'm gonna get me my civil rights, [3x]
   Gonna sit, *etc.*

I'm gonna sit down at Woolworth's counter [3x]
   Gonna sit, *etc.*

As new problems, new threats, new concerns arise, there will be new songs for people to sing. Don't ever underestimate the power of a song. It sometimes brings about more changes than a law or a bullet. The British scholar, Andrew Fletcher, wrote in 1703, "Give me the making of the songs of a nation and I care not who makes its laws."

CHAPTER FOUR

Instruments
of Folk Music

What instrument pops into your head when you think of folk music?

The guitar? Almost everyone thinks of the guitar as *the* folk instrument.

But do you know that the Hottentots in Africa accompany their folk music by shaking rattles made by sewing pebbles into dried antelope ears? That some Mexican folk dancers tie bundles of butterflies to their

This primitive Mexican folk instrument is both a rattle and a whistle.

ankles to make a soft, whirring sound as they dance? That among the North American Indians, some folk songs are sung to the beat of deer bones tied to the dancers' legs? That some tribes in the South American jungle tap on inflated jaguar eyes to give a beat to their folk music?

Some folk instruments are made of human bones.

The idea of using bones—human or animal—for musical instruments goes back very far in history. These reindeer-bone flutes, which were found in a cave in Czechoslovakia, are about 30,000 years old.

In 1805, an English traveler in Paraguay told of seeing flutes carved from the bones of Spanish missionaries killed by the Indians. There are also accounts of human skulls being used as drums in Mexico. And the Brazilian National Museum has a trumpet with a skull as the bell.

Even though folk music is mostly singing music, folk instruments are important. Antelope-ear and jaguar-eye instruments do exist, to be sure, but they are not the most popular instruments. The most popular instruments are the guitar, the banjo, and the dulcimer.

All three of these instruments developed from the oldest and simplest of string instruments, the string bow. This instrument started as nothing more than the bow used to shoot arrows. When you pull the tight string and let go, you hear a pleasant, soft "ping." Some early player of the string bow had the idea of resting one end of the bow on his teeth with his mouth open. This made the sound louder by adding the resonance of his open mouth.

In one of the oldest forms of the string bow, the end of the string is tied to the top of a short, limber tree. The other end is attached to a section of bark over a hole in the ground. The hole adds resonance, making the sound of the plucked string much louder.

The guitar itself has a long history. Its name comes from *kithara*, a leading string instrument in ancient

[55]

This painting on an ancient Greek vase shows a woman playing a *kithara*, one of the ancestors of the guitar.

Greece, some ten thousand years ago. The *kithara* had a hollow wooden soundbox, with two curved arms rising from it. A crossbar connected the two arms near their tops. A number of strings, from five to eleven, ran from the soundbox to the crossbar. The players accompanied their singing by plucking the strings of the *kithara*.

A three-thousand-year-old carving from the region near modern-day Syria shows an instrument more like today's guitar. It is a hollow-bodied instrument, with curved sides, a flat top and back, and a long neck over which the strings are stretched. This guitar-like instrument was introduced into Spain by the Moors of North Africa about eight hundred years

Terpsichore, the muse of dance, is seen playing a guitar in this 15th century Italian drawing.

TERPSICORE · XIII·

ago. A carving in a church in Spain, from the year 1188, shows a four-string instrument almost identical to the modern guitar. By the sixteenth century, the Spanish guitar had the standard six strings.

From Spain, the guitar spread throughout the rest of Europe. Spanish settlers also packed guitars with their other belongings, and brought them to North and South America. The Spanish guitar was soon known and played in many places around the world.

Although there is a standard six-string guitar, some performers use guitars with anywhere from four to twelve strings. Leadbelly, one of the greatest folk musicians of recent times, was known as the king of twelve-string guitar players.

Ellen Jenkins, a popular folk singer and teacher, often uses a four-string guitar when she plays and sings. (Photo courtesy Folkways Records)

Folk singers also use guitars in different shapes and sizes, made out of different kinds of woods or even plastic. The strings can be metal, nylon, or gut. They may be plucked by the player's fingers, or with a plastic or metal pick or plectrum. And there is no limit to the variety of strums and accompaniments that a guitar player can use.

The basic principle of all guitars is the same. The player plucks a string to set it into vibration. The vibrating string produces the sound of the guitar.

All the strings on the guitar are the same length. If you look closely, though, you will see that the higher-pitched strings are thinner and tighter than the lower-pitched ones. The thinner and tighter the string, the higher the note it produces.

The player can change the vibrating length of the string by pressing it down with a finger. This pushes the string against one of the frets, the strips of metal set in the fingerboard, and stops the vibrations at that point. The shorter the vibrating length, the higher the pitch.

Sometimes the player finds it easier to play a particular song if all the strings are made shorter for the entire piece. The player does this by clamping a *capo tasto* to the neck. The *capo*, as most players call it, presses all the strings down on one fret, making them all shorter, and therefore higher in pitch.

When the slaves were brought to America in the

early days of our country, they brought their African music with them. The songs they carried to these shores are now all but forgotten. However, one of the instruments that they brought is still popular today. The early slaves called it a "bania." In 1782, Thomas Jefferson wrote that the chief instrument of the slaves was a "banjar." Today we know it as the banjo.

Most scholars think that the *bania* was an African form of the guitar. The instrument is shaped something like a lollipop. The round, sucking part of the lollipop is the soundbox. It is made of a round, wooden hoop, with an animal skin stretched over it. The stick of the lollipop is the neck of the banjo. The early banjo usually had three strings stretched over the neck and soundbox.

A Virginia farmer, Joel Walker Sweeney, was among the first white men to learn to play the banjo. He made some improvements, too, adding a fourth and then a fifth string. Sweeney introduced the instrument to white audiences throughout the South. Other players were attracted by the exciting sound of the banjo, and a banjo craze spread throughout the country. From about the 1880s through the 1920s, the four-string banjo was a part of almost every ragtime or jazz band. The five-string banjo, though, was largely ignored.

In our time, however, the five-string banjo is making a comeback, while the four-string instrument

The farm laborer plays his banjo while his wife reads the Bible in their government-built cottage, in Caldwell, Idaho, 1941. (Photo by Lee, courtesy Library of Congress)

has faded. Such outstanding performers as Earl Scruggs and Pete Seeger are responsible for the new interest in the five-stringer. Their banjos have thin white calf-skin, or vellum, stretched over the metal or hardwood hoop of the soundbox. The neck is a hard wood, such as walnut or mahogany, with a black ebony finger-board. Though most banjos have frets, like a guitar, some folk music players prefer fretless banjos. They like to be able to slide from note to note, and to play the notes between the frets.

In recent years, another string instrument has been growing popular among folk musicians. This instrument dates back some five thousand years to the area around what is now Iran. Its ancient name was *santir*. Today we call it a dulcimer. The name comes from

Dennis Dorogi polishes the back of a tear-drop shaped dulcimer that he has just finished making in his Brocton, New York, workshop. (Photo by Melvin Berger)

[62]

the Latin words *dulce melos,* meaning "sweet song." It is a sweet-sounding instrument, well-suited to playing the melody lines of simple folk songs.

There are two types of dulcimers. The hammered dulcimer is built on a flat soundbox in the shape of a trapezoid, which looks like a triangle with the top cut off. It has strings of various lengths stretched across the soundbox. The player strikes the strings with curved wooden hammers to set them into vibration. While being played, the hammered dulcimer is placed on a table, on the player's lap, or is hung from a strap around the neck. The hammered dulcimer is quite popular in several areas of Europe. The Hungarian gypsies are famous for the use they make of the hammered dulcimer in their folk music.

The more popular American dulcimer is called either the plucked, mountain, or Appalachian dulcimer. Sometimes you will even hear it called a whamadiddle! This dulcimer is usually shaped like an hourglass or like a teardrop. It is smaller than the hammered model. Instead of using hammers to set the strings into vibration, the player plucks them with finger, feather quills, or almost anything else that is handy.

Most plucked dulcimers have either three or four strings. In many four-string dulcimers, the fourth string is tuned to the same note as one of the three strings. The performer usually plays the melody of the

[63]

song he or she is singing on one of the strings. The other strings are used as a drone accompaniment that stays the same for the whole song.

Perhaps the dulcimer is becoming popular because it is rather inexpensive to buy and is easy to learn to play. Dennis Dorogi, a fine dulcimer maker, finds that many of the new players are city people, rather than the country folk who have a tradition of dulcimer playing.

The modern washtub bass is similar to the string bow tied to a tree. A broomstick replaces the tree. An upturned washtub replaces the hole in the ground. The broomstick is held with one end resting on the edge of the washtub. The string runs from the top of the broomstick to the center of the tub. The player's left hand raises and lowers the broomstick, which tightens or loosens the string. The looser the string, the lower the pitch; the tighter the string, the higher the pitch. The player's right hand is used to pluck the string.

The string instruments of folk music developed gradually over many thousands of years. Some of the other folk instruments came to life in a shorter time, and much more recently.

The harmonica, or mouth organ, was invented in the year 1829. The instrument is in the shape of a flat, wooden box, divided into narrow channels by thin, wooden slats. A small sliver of metal or cane, called a reed, is set in each channel.

[64]

The washtub bass is often played with other instruments, such as the violin and guitar. The player stands with one foot on the washtub, holding the broomstick with his left hand and plucking the string with his right hand. (Illustration by Robert Galster).

When the player blows into that channel, the reed vibrates, producing a single tone. Since each reed is a different size, each one gives a different pitch. Improvements in the harmonica make it possible to play more than one note at a time, to sound one note blowing and another drawing or sucking, and to increase the total number of notes that can be played.

The accordion, or squeeze box, looks nothing like the harmonica. Yet the two instruments are closely related. They were both invented in 1829. Players on both instruments produce the sound by setting reeds into vibration. The harmonica player blows on the reeds. The accordion player pushes and pulls the bellows of the instrument, forcing air past the reeds.

The accordion player presses the keys of the piano-like keyboard with the fingers of the right hand to get the individual notes. The fingers of the left hand press buttons to sound entire chords, which provide harmony for the right-hand melodies.

The steel drum, an even more modern folk instrument, was created just after World War II on the island of Trinidad. Trinidad has a rather large oil-drilling industry, and there are plenty of fifty-five-gallon oil drums around. The idea of using them as drums came, it is said, from someone's attempt to hammer out a dent in his garbage can. As he hammered, he noticed that it produced a musical tone. Later he found that banging on the end of an oil drum sounded even better. And thus a new musical instrument, the steel drum, was born.

The players call their steel drums "pans." They make their pans from the end sections of these large

The accordion player pushes and pulls the bellows of her instrument to produce the sound. This performer is leading a song at a union meeting in Bristow, Oklahoma, in 1940. (Photo by Lee, courtesy Library of Congress)

The different sections of the top of the steel drum are hammered to various thicknesses so the player can get different notes when she strikes them with the sticks. (Photo by Melvin Berger, courtesy Calliope's Children Steel Orchestra)

oil drums. The pans are hammered to make the metal thin in certain places. The thinner the metal, the higher the pitch. The player strikes the hammered metal sections with a rubber knob on a stick. Three to eight drums, with different sections hammered to various thicknesses, give the players a full scale of notes.

The list of folk instruments goes on and on. There are melody instruments, like the violin (folk musicians call it a fiddle, but it is exactly the same as a concert violin) and the recorder (a type of flute, held straight down instead of across the player's lips). There are all sorts of percussion instruments, from the talking drums of Africa to Southern street musicians clacking two spoons against their thighs.

Some of the instruments are old, some are new. Some were borrowed from the concert hall, others from the kitchen. Some can be mastered in fifteen minutes, others need years of study. Perhaps this is the greatest wonder of the folk instruments—their great variety, and the many ways in which they are used to make folk music around the world.

The recorder is related to the flute. It is quite easy to play, and is a wonderful instrument for playing folk music. (Photo by Melvin Berger)

[68]

A father-and-son team of country fiddlers is seen playing in their Iron River, Michigan, home in this 1937 photograph. (Photo by Lee, courtesy Library of Congress)

CHAPTER FIVE

The Science of Folk Music

In the year 1882, a group of Bellacoola Indians from the Pacific coast of Canada performed their tribal songs and dances in a concert hall in Berlin, Germany. They caused a sensation. The audiences were fascinated by the strange-sounding music.

One of their admirers was Carl Stumpf, a philosopher, musician and scholar. Professor Stumpf decided to copy down the most attractive Indian songs. He asked the performers to sing the songs over and over. Slowly, note by note, he copied down what he heard. Later he studied the music. He wrote articles describing it, and comparing it with the more familiar music of the time. It was the first time anyone had thought of studying folk music in this scholarly way.

Much later, the term "ethnomusicology" was coined to describe the scientific study of the folk music and primitive music of different cultures. The word comes from *ethno*, meaning a culture or a people, *music*, originally the art of the Muse, and *ology*, the science of.

Today's ethnomusicologists spend time in the field, recording examples of folk music from all over the world. Then, at their desks, they write out the music in standard musical notation and study the music they have collected.

This 1910 photograph shows an ethnomusicologist collecting songs in a village in Europe.

The single most important tool of the eth-nomusicologists is the portable, battery-operated tape recorder. No longer do they have to ask a singer, called an informant, to do a song over and over again until they have copied it all down. No longer do they need an electric generator and heavy, bulky recording equipment. A small, light tape recorder is easily carried everywhere, and makes possible the collecting of songs that would have been virtually impossible in the past.

And it's a good thing, too! With each passing day, the folk songs of the people in many places in the world become harder to capture. As the older generations die out, so do many very beautiful songs. Once they are lost, they are gone forever. Many younger people are not interested in learning the songs from the past, which they consider old-fashioned. Also, folk music is losing ground to popular and commercial music. There are few spots left on earth without radios and phonographs blaring out the latest hit tunes.

Doing field work in ethnomusicolgy involves much more than riding a jeep from village to village, recording songs on a tape recorder, and then heading home to write them out. Collecting folk songs involves learning all that you can about the culture of the people in that region. Very often this means living in a village for weeks, or even months, to get to know the people and their way of life and to gain their confidence. It means getting answers to many questions: What is the meaning of the song; what function does it serve; what activities does it accompany? Where did the informant learn the song? Who made it up? Which are considered the best songs and the best singers? Why? How much music from outside the culture have the people heard? How has it influenced their folk music? Are the songs performed by a single singer, or does the group join in? Who decides who the song leaders are? How much of the song is fixed and unchanging? What parts change with each performance?

Perhaps the hardest part of the ethnomusicologist's job is done at home. Transcribing the songs from the tapes into musical notation is a necessary first step in the serious study of a piece of music. It takes from one to two hours to transcribe a one-minute song. The scholar plays the tape over many times, writing the music down note by note. There are frequent stops to add a note, or to correct a note, until the whole song is down on paper.

The difficulties are enormous. Most informants are elderly. Their voices are weak and they often sing badly out of tune. Many of the songs do not use our regular scales and have melodic and rhythmic schemes that do not sound familiar. There is a great danger that the scholar will write down what he or she expects to hear, instead of what is actually heard. The recordings are seldom of very high quality. It is a wonder that the songs are ever written down at all.

The ethnomusicologists collect most of their songs from older people. In this photograph an elderly woman is seen scraping out a tune on the violin that she remembers from when she was a child. (Photo courtesy Library of Congress)

When the song is finally transcribed, the ethnomusicologist starts to study the music and the words: Does the song use the regular major or minor scales, or does it use a different tone system? How many different notes appear in the song? Does the melody repeat itself; are there contrasting melodies; are there variations on the melody? Do the rhythms fall into the usual beats and measures; do the rhythmic patterns repeat; are there contrasts and variations of tempo or rhythm?

The words are studied for meaning, language, how they are set to music, and so on. The ethnomusicologists compare each song with songs from the same and from different cultures. The similarities and the differences are examined. They write reports describing the song, comparing it with others, and explaining its special features.

For example, scholars discovered that European folk songs very often were better preserved in America than in the countries from which they had come. Cecil Sharp, the English folk song collector, visited America in the early years of this century. He heard many old English folk songs from descendants of English settlers living in the southern Appalachian Mountains of Virginia, North Carolina, Tennessee, and Kentucky. These songs, amazingly enough, were no longer being sung in England.

Folk songs along the outside or fringes of a culture, it seems, survive longer than songs at the center of the culture. That is why the English songs are remembered better among some Americans descended from the English settlers than by the English themselves.

Likewise, music from a fringe area tells a lot about folk music that existed at the center of a culture. The present two-part folk music sung in harmony in the fringe country of Iceland and in the Caucasus Mountains of Russia is believed to be all that is left of the ancient folk music of central Europe. The more modern folk music from central Europe that we know is mostly for solo singer, and has but one melody.

Ethnomusicologists also believe that if the music of two distant cultures is very similar, it is more than coincidence. Either the two cultures had a common origin and later separated, or they lived together over a long period of time. These conclusions often coincide with discoveries made by anthropologists, scientists who study man and his culture.

The folk music of some tribes in eastern Siberia is very similar to the music of the Eskimos who live in Alaska and northern Canada. The songs of both people have rather large jumps in the melody, often skipping three or four notes. In both cultures the songs are sung with a very tight, strained vocal quality. And both have a single melody line over a sung accompaniment. In fact, the folk music of the North American Eskimos is much more like the music of Asia than the music of Europe or Africa.

From this evidence, some ethnomusicologists hold that the Siberians and the Eskimos were probably one people long, long ago. This fits the anthropologists' belief that the North American Eskimos came over from Asia about fifty thousand years ago by way of the Bering Strait, which reaches from Siberia in Asia across to Alaska.

Jack and Anna Kilpatrick are modern ethnomusicologists. The many songs that they have uncovered and collected have increased our understanding of the wonderful variety of folk music in various cultures.

The Kilpatricks came across a very beautiful Indian song in 1964. Their informant was a Cherokee medicine man. He sang this song for them as he applied paint to his body before a dance. He repeated the song four times as he painted his forehead, nose, chin, cheeks, and chest, using a cardinal feather to apply the paint. The song, he later explained, has the power to charm and attract women.

The Kilpatricks studied the song. They found that some of the words were in the language of the Natchez tribe of the Muskogee Indians, who lived among the Cherokees. They researched the origins and meanings of the words in the song and found the words that gave the song its magical powers. The transcribed song was published, along with the information they had collected on the background and meaning of the song. Here is the song as they prepared it:

Some people say that ethnomusicologists dig up music in the field only to bury it in the library. The fact is, though, that these folk-music experts have saved hundreds of songs that otherwise would have been lost and forgotten. They made them available to folk singers and performers all over the world. Through the songs they have collected, we have greatly increased our understanding of the music, the cultures, and the ways of life of different peoples.

CHAPTER SIX

Folk and Art Music: The Twin Streams

Folk music is one stream in the life and culture of a people. Art music, music that is written by trained, professional composers and performed by trained, professional musicians, is another. The two streams run side by side. At times they come together and meet. Other times they separate and flow away from each other.

Going back to the eighth and ninth centuries, we find folk and art music joining together in the music of the Mass, which is the principal service of the Catholic Church. Five parts of the Mass are sung. In those days, the Kyrie, Gloria, and Agnus Dei parts of the Mass came from old church chants. The Credo and Sanctus, though, were based on folk songs. They were, and still are, simpler and more direct.

Over the following centuries, folk music and art

music drifted apart. The folk music was in the language of the people and was based on major and minor scales. It usually had strong beats so that it could be used for dancing. And the words dealt with subjects that were of interest to the people.

Most of the art music was church music. It was in Latin, and used the church modes, which are special scales that sound somewhat strange to our ears. The church music followed the free-flowing, unaccented rhythms of the church chants. And the words of the church music were always on religious topics.

Folk music and art music began to come together again in the fifteenth century. It seems to us now that art music moved toward folk music. Composers of art music began to use the scales and rhythms of folk music, and to borrow folk melodies for their works.

Dozens of composers around this time used a French folk song, "L'Homme Armé" for their Masses and other compositions. The words of "L'Homme Armé" have been lost, but here is the melody:

L'HOMME ARMÉ

In the following century, Martin Luther, the leader of the Protestant Reformation, was a great admirer of folk songs. He wanted to see them widely used in the newly formed Protestant Churches.

Luther, who was also a fine musician, took many old German folk melodies, and set new words to them to create the first Protestant chorales and hymns. These works became the core of music in the Protestant Churches.

Folk music and art music came together, too, in the highly popular ballad operas of the early eighteenth century. New words were written to old folk ballads and other familiar tunes. They were then strung together to make an opera. The subjects were the common people, rather than the gods and goddesses found in the typical operas of the day. In *The Beggar's Opera,* perhaps the most famous ballad opera, the original words were written by John Gay; the sixty-nine tunes were collected and arranged by John Christopher Pepusch.

By the year 1800, folk and art music began to go their separate ways again. But there is almost no composer since then who was not influenced by the folk music he heard.

Here, as an example, is the beginning of the last movement of Franz Joseph Haydn's Symphony No. 104:

HAYDN'S SYMPHONY #104

Franz Joseph Haydn

And here is a bit of a folk song, "Oj Jellena," from Croatia, the area in central Europe of Haydn's birthplace:

OJ JELLENA

Croatian Folk Song

Is the similarity a coincidence? Probably not. The best explanation is that Haydn was influenced, consciously or unconsciously, by the folk music that surrounded him. The music of almost every composer shows some traces of the melodies and rhythms of his nation's folk music.

A number of composers are so deeply steeped in folk music that among their compositions are works

that sound as though they are based on folk songs—
even though the music is completely original. Aaron
Copland in America, Béla Bartók in Hungary, Ralph
Vaughan Williams in England, and Jean Sibelius in
Finland are such composers.

In some cases, melodies created by composers are
so much like folk melodies that people mistakenly
think they are authentic folk songs. Have you ever
sung this melody, thinking it was a folk song?

It is not a folk song at all. It is the theme that
Beethoven composed for the last movement of his
Ninth Symphony.

What about the well-known Negro spiritual
"Goin' Home"?

GOIN' HOME

Antonín Dvořák

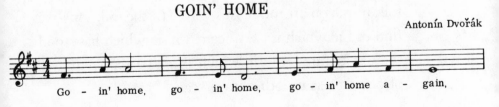

Go - in' home, go - in' home, go - in' home a - gain,

[83]

Originally, the melody was the theme of the second movement of Antonín Dvořák's New World Symphony. Words were added later, and only then did it become popular as a spiritual.

Many composers used folk melodies in their composed works as a way of expressing love for their country. Brahms in Germany, Grieg in Norway, De Falla in Spain, Chopin in Poland, Liszt in Hungary, Tchaikovsky in Russia, Smetana in Bohemia (now Czechoslovakia), and many others borrowed actual folk melodies for their symphonies and operas. "The Beech Tree" is a good example of a Russian folk song which Tchaikovsky borrowed to use as the last movement theme in his Fourth Symphony.

THE BEECH TREE

Peter Ilyich Tchaikovsky

Ralph Vaughan Williams, the British composer and folk music collector, explained the influence of folk music on art music this way: "In the folk song we find music which is . . . sincere, music which has stood the test of time, music which must be representative of our race as no other music can."

[84]

CHAPTER SEVEN

Folk Music in Our Time

The number of folk singers, guitar pickers, and song makers has never been greater than today. They vary from folk-music performers singing and playing on records, radio, and television, or at large folk festivals, to people getting together to swap songs just for fun. And for each one of these people making his or her own music, there are many, many more who enjoy listening to folk music.

Why are so many people interested in folk music?

There are many reasons: Young people and students find folk music is music they enjoy, that they can make themselves, and that expresses their feelings and beliefs about the world.

Pop-music performers also learned how to present folk music in a very attractive and appealing way. They introduced folk music to immense audiences

[85]

The interest in folk music has never been greater than today. Many folk music performers, such as The Browns, are making recordings. (Photo courtesy RCA Records)

through recordings, radio and television appearances, and live concerts.

In their search for roots and identities, many people are turning to folk music as a way to find themselves. To the growing numbers of people who have adopted do-it-yourself as a way of life, the idea

[86]

of sitting at a concert or in front of a radio and listening to music does not seem very appealing. They want do-it-yourself music, which is, of course, folk music.

Over the last seventy years or so, there have also been several outstanding folk musicians collecting, creating, and performing folk songs. They brought the beauties and pleasures of folk music to vast numbers of people. Their important contributions led directly to the great surge of folk-music activity in our time.

The pioneers in the growth of interest in American folk music are the father and son team of John and Alan Lomax. Since 1910, they have collected and preserved thousands of songs from America's past and present.

John Lomax (1867-1948) grew up near the Chisholm Trail in Texas. After his graduation from Harvard in 1907, he set out to collect the folk songs of the southwest part of the country. The result was *Cowboy Songs,* published in 1910. It included the first printed version of songs like "Home on the Range," "Git Along, Little Dogies," and "The Old Chisholm Trail," among many others.

John's son, Alan (b. 1915), joined his father in the 1930s. They traveled widely in the South and West, collecting and recording all the folk songs they could find. These records became the foundation of the largest and best collection of American folk music, the Archives of American Folk Song at the Library of Congress in Washington, D.C. There are about one hundred thousand records of songs, some made in the field, some made in professional recording studios. Besides the recordings, the Archives contain a wealth of books, articles, and related material on folk music for ethnomusicologists, folk music performers, and others to explore.

Yet Alan does not consider the Archives the Lomaxes' most important contribution to folk music. He is proudest that they brought two of the greatest American folk musicians, Leadbelly and Woody Guthrie, to the attention of the American public.

John and Alan Lomax met Huddie Leadbetter, nicknamed Leadbelly, while collecting songs at the penitentiary in Angola, Louisiana. Born in 1885, in Mooringsport, Louisiana, Leadbelly was often in trouble and just as often in jail. When the Lomaxes met him that hot summer day in 1933, Leadbelly was serving a sentence on a charge of murder.

As a child, Leadbelly had learned to play the harmonica, accordion, and piano. But his favorite instrument was the twelve-string guitar. His fingers danced over the strings with a thumb pick and a long steel finger pick, while his rich, powerful voice rang out over the driving rhythms that he played. "I'm the king of all the twelve-string guitar players of the

Alan Lomax, along with his father, John, has collected and
preserved thousands of songs from America's past and present.
(Photograph courtesy Alan Lomax)

world," he would proudly say. And no one ever disputed this.

The Lomaxes asked Leadbelly to sing for them. He was more than willing. Song after song poured into their brand-new portable recording equipment. The first song they recorded was one that Leadbelly had learned from his uncle. The song, "Goodnight Irene," later became one of the biggest folk-music hits

Leadbelly was a prisoner in Louisiana when he was discovered by John and Alan Lomax. They brought his remarkable talent as a creator and performer of folk songs to the attention of the American people.

of all time. Its success, however, came six months after Leadbelly died.

Leadbelly sang and sang for them. Then he asked the Lomaxes for a favor. Would they record a song that he had composed and play it for Governor O. K. Allen of Louisiana? It was an appeal for his own pardon.

I left my wife wringin' her hands 'n' cryin',
"Governor O. K. Allen, save this man of mine."

The next day the Lomaxes took the appeal to Governor Allen. One year later, two-time convicted murderer Leadbelly was paroled to the custody of the Lomaxes. Together they traveled through the South, visiting many prisons, singing for the inmates, and recording the songs of the prisoners.

Later, the Lomaxes and Leadbelly performed for audiences in Washington, Philadelphia, and New York. The city crowds applauded wildly as Leadbelly sang his favorites—"Goodnight Irene," "Rock Island Line," "Midnight Special," and "Kisses Sweeter than Wine." They were fascinated by this simple, honest man, who was able to bring such beautiful and exciting southern country songs to the sophisticated people of these northern cities.

After this, Leadbelly settled in New York, giving

[91]

concerts and making recordings. The legacy he left when he died in 1949 included all the songs he had made up. It also included the evidence that audiences all over could enjoy and be moved by real folk songs from the farms, jails, sailing ships, and work gangs of America.

The Lomaxes helped bring another great folk musician to the American public. Woodrow Wilson Guthrie, always known as Woody Guthrie, was born in Okemah, Oklahoma, in 1912. He learned music from his father who played guitar and banjo in several cowboy bands. Woody had just thirteen years to grow up before his world collapsed around him. Within one year, his father's real estate business failed, his sister was killed in an explosion, and his mother was committed to the State Asylum for the Insane.

Young Woody took to the road—picking grapes, drilling wells, building houses, hauling wood, and plowing fields. Nights he took his harmonica to dance halls, pool halls, and even street corners where he played for nickels from the crowd. Later he played his guitar at dances and for traveling medicine shows.

By 1935, Woody had drifted to California. There were many other "Okies" there who had fled the Oklahoma Dust Bowl. He earned a small living playing and singing in saloons and union halls, for parties, and on radio shows. The songs he sang were

Woody Guthrie is one of the greatest folk musicians that
America has produced. (Photo by Robin Carson, courtesy
Woody Guthrie Publications, Inc.)

ballads he had learned from his mother, blues from his father, and many songs he himself made up.

Woody could not stay in one place for long. He was always on the road, crisscrossing back and forth all over the country. Eventually, though, he settled in New York City. But it was a rough time. Not many people wanted to hear folk singers in those days. He finally landed a good paying job on a radio station. After a month, though, he quit because he could not stand the songs he was being asked to sing.

But Woody kept on singing wherever he could. He made a few records and appeared from time to time on radio shows. All the while he kept on composing, turning out a glorious succession of new songs. Hardly a day went by that Woody did not write a song. "This Land Is Your Land" and "So Long" are just two of the thousand or so songs he wrote. He never became very famous or made much money. In the world of folk music, though, he was looked up to as one of the leading and most important figures of the time.

In 1950, at the age of thirty-eight, Woody began to have dizzy spells and to feel weak. These are the first symptoms of a wasting sickness, called Huntington's disease. He entered the hospital in 1952, and remained there until his death in 1967. But Woody's influence lives on. Many of today's most outstanding folk singers call themselves "Woody's Children." It is a wonderful and fitting tribute to one of America's greatest folk musicians.

At midnight on the night of March 13, 1940, there was a folk-music concert at the Broadway Theater in New York City. It was to raise money for the migrant farm workers in California. The performers included the leading folk musicians of the day, Leadbelly, Woody Guthrie, Alan Lomax, and many others. There was also a youngster making his first public appearance as a folk singer. His name was Pete Seeger.

Pete Seeger arrived before this large audience via an entirely different route from Woody or Leadbelly. Pete Seeger was born into a comfortable family of musicians in New York City in 1919. Pete's father was an ethnomusicologist who taught at the Juilliard School of Music in New York. His mother, a fine violinist, also taught at Juilliard. Pete attended private schools and Harvard University. He had all the advantages of being part of a successful and musical family.

Pete started to play the ukelele when he was eight years old, and used to accompany himself when he sang in school. By the time he was fifteen, he was also playing the banjo in the school jazz band. One year later Pete made the wonderful discovery that the five-string banjo was his favorite instrument.

That summer, Pete's father took him along on a

song-collecting trip to the Asheville Folk Festival in North Carolina. Pete was excited by the great sound of the country banjo players. He was struck by the meaning and beauty of their folk songs. He decided to work hard on the five-string banjo and to learn as much about folk music as he could.

Still, the idea of becoming a professional folk singer had not occurred to Pete. He went to Harvard University, but left after two years. He studied painting. Then he got a job at the Library of Congress, working with Alan Lomax. Along came Woody Guthrie who convinced Seeger that the only way to learn folk music was by traveling, meeting folks, and singing songs.

So Pete left his job in Washington, and went on the road with Woody, traveling in Woody's beat-up, old car. After a while, Pete struck off on his own. He hitchhiked and rode empty freight cars all over the country.

Finally he arrived back in New York City. He was offered his first paid engagement. Would he sing for the children in a school for five dollars? "It seemed like stealing," Pete writes, "to take money for something I'd always done for fun." But he did. Some time later he appeared on the stage of the Broadway Theater with Leadbelly and Guthrie. Pete Seeger was launched on a career as a professional folk singer.

Pete Seeger has a magical ability to put over a folk song. He is a great popular success wherever he sings. (Photo by Lyn Adler, courtesy Harold Leventhal)

From the very beginning, there was never any question of Pete's magical ability to put across a song. Wherever he sings, in concerts all over the world, on college campuses, at union meetings, on records, radio, television, and movies, for every age from nursery school to senior citizens, Pete wins over his audience. They listen intently. Before long, they are clapping and singing along with him.

With two friends who were active in the labor union movement, Lee Hays and Millard Lampell, Pete formed the Almanac Singers in 1940. (Lee Hays explained the name: Every house in the country has two books—the Bible for the next world, the Almanac for this.) For a year and a half a parade of folk singers, including Woody Guthrie, drifted in and out of the group. Of the informal structure of the Almanac Singers, Guthrie wrote, "They are the only group that rehearses on stage."

After serving in World War II, Pete Seeger, along with Lee Hays, Fred Hellerman, and Ronnie Gilbert, formed The Weavers, one of the most successful folk music groups of all times. They satisfied those who wanted their music pure by staying close to the words, music, and spirit of the folk song. They also pleased those used to the sounds of pop music by working out clever and attractive arrangements of the music. The Weavers' recording of Leadbelly's "Goodnight Irene"

After World War II, Ronnie Gilbert, Pete Seeger (playing banjo), Lee Hays and Fred Hellerman (playing guitar) formed The Weavers, giving a new popularity to folk music. (Photo courtesy Harold Leventhal)

[99]

sold about two million copies, the first hit folk-music record.

Pete Seeger's fans admire him both as a musician and as a person. In 1955, Pete was called before the House Un-American Activities Committee as part of their investigation of subversives in the United States. Seeger refused to answer questions about his personal beliefs, saying that these were not proper questions to put to any American. He also refused to answer questions on the beliefs of people whom he knew. Steadfastly he upheld the rights and principles in which he believes.

For these actions, Pete Seeger was cited for contempt of Congress in 1961, and sentenced to one year in jail. The conviction was reversed within one hour. But Pete's career suffered a setback. Over the following years, radio and television stations, recording and movie companies, and even many concert promoters would not hire him.

By the end of the 1960s, however, the political and social climate in America had changed. Pete Seeger was accepted once again. His fame and stature grew even greater than before. By now many consider him the best folk singer of our time.

During these same years the civil rights movement and the protests against the war in Vietnam were spreading throughout the country. Out of these

[100]

struggles came a host of young, politically concerned, as well as politically active, folk singers. They include Joan Baez, Phil Ochs, Paul Simon and Art Garfunkel, Tom Paxton, Judy Collins, and Tim Hardin. But, of them all, perhaps Bob Dylan best expresses the concerns and beliefs of the time. His songs succeed in bringing the folk-music traditions of America's past right up to the present.

We know that Bob Dylan was born as Bob Zimmerman, in 1941, near Minneapolis, Minnesota. Later he changed his name to Dylan Thomas to show his admiration for the Welsh poet of that name. Still later, he arrived at the name Bob Dylan.

Bob Dylan was involved with folk music from his very early days. As a youngster, Bob played guitar and wrote poems. While at the University of Minnesota, he frequently appeared at campus coffee houses. Then, after leaving the University in 1960, he came to the New York area, performing in Greenwich Village bars, restaurants, and coffee houses. But most important were his frequent visits with Woody Guthrie, who was already hospitalized. Along with many other folk singers, Bob Dylan learned a great deal from Guthrie.

Word quickly spread in New York's folk-music circles about the shy, curly-haired folk singer from out West. He did not play guitar or harmonica very

In his music, Bob Dylan sums up many of the concerns and beliefs of young people. (Photo courtesy Columbia Records)

Joan Baez is one of the outstanding young, politically concerned folk singers that came to public attention in the 1960s. (Photo courtesy Vanguard Records)

[103]

well, he sang out of tune sometimes, and he had a somewhat nasal voice quality. But he had a sense of poetry, a sense of music, a social awareness, and a performing style that gave his songs a meaning and message for teen-agers that no other performer could equal.

In 1962, Bob Dylan wrote one of his greatest songs, "Blowin' in the Wind." It became an immense hit. People may argue that it is or is not a folk song. But it is generally considered to be part of the folk music of the sixties and seventies, as are the other Dylan songs, including "Masters of War," "The Times They Are A-Changin'," and "Mr. Tambourine Man."

The new folk songs by Bob Dylan and the others made the mindless words of the rock 'n' roll songs that were popular at the time seem particularly silly and meaningless. The rock 'n' roll groups began to imitate the young new folk singers. They made the words of their songs more important. They sang about subjects with greater meaning. The rock 'n' roll music grew up; it came of age. To mark this change, people began to call this new type of music "rock," instead of "rock 'n' roll."

At the same time, the rock sound was influencing the new folk music. The exciting beat of rock began to appear in the songs of Dylan and the others. The singers used rock bands for their accompaniments.

The electric guitar was accepted as an instrument of folk music.

All this back and forth influence led to the birth of a new style of music, called folk-rock. It combined some of the age-old qualities of folk music with the most up-to-date sounds and approaches of the rock style.

Some of the better-known folk-rock performers today are Joni Mitchell, John Denver, and Carly Simon. But these names may be different tomorrow, as new stars come forward, and some of the old ones fade.

Folk music joined with rock to create folk-rock. But rock is only one type of modern popular music. Folk music joined with a different style of pop music to create what is called either country and western, bluegrass, mountain, or hillbilly music. Some of the popular performers of this music are Eddy Arnold, Johnny Cash, Chet Atkins, Earl Scruggs, and Lester Flatt.

Country and western songs are mostly written by commercial composers trying to capture the direct, simple qualities of folk music. The melodies and rhythms are usually very straightforward, with a heavy, accented beat. The harmonies are traditional. Rock composers and performers are much more willing to experiment, and to search for new sounds and new effects.

In general, the words of country songs deal with love, and other subjects similar to those of folk music. While there are plenty of folk-rock love songs, there are also a good number of folk-rock songs on events and ideas of national or international importance.

It is very hard for us to tell how folk-rock and country and western music will fit in with the folk-music tradition. Will they be considered the "new" folk music? Will they become part of the change and growth of folk music? Will they be seen as products of commercial, popular composers who used the ideas of folk music for their inspiration?

It is hard to say. But time will surely tell.

Chet Atkins is a leading performer of country and western music. This style grew out of America's folk music tradition. (Photo courtesy RCA Records)

Folk-rock combines aspects of folk music with the sounds and instruments of modern rock music. John Denver is one of the better-known folk-rock performers. (Photo courtesy RCA Records)

CHAPTER EIGHT

Folk Music and You

Listening to folk music is great fun. Reading about folk music can be interesting. But neither can compare to the pleasure of doing-it-yourself—singing folk songs, playing folk instruments, and making up folk songs.

When you begin, you may sing out of tune and hit wrong notes on your instrument. Perhaps you will feel that your original songs sound silly. But try it anyhow. Making your own folk music can be hard work. But being able to sing and play for others and to hear your own songs makes it very worthwhile.

If you can read music, it is easy to learn songs from published collections of folk songs. There are many excellent folk-song books in libraries. Some are available in paperback editions at low cost. If you have a good ear and can imagine what the printed notes will sound like, you might be able to sing the melodies right away. If not, try them out first on a piano or any other instrument that you play, to get the melody. Some folk-song books come with records of the songs. You can then learn the songs that way.

While you can sing folk songs without accompaniment, most people prefer to sing *and* play. Band and orchestra instruments are fine for playing folk tunes and dances, but it is usually impossible to play one of these instruments and sing at the same time.

Several high school students got together to form Calliope's Children, a steel drum orchestra. They are enjoying the thrill of playing folk songs, and other music, together. (Photo by Melvin Berger, courtesy Calliope's Children Steel Orchestra)

The easiest accompanying instrument is the autoharp. Most autoharps have about thirty-six strings. Wooden bars, marked with the names of the different chords, are in place over the strings. To sound a C chord, the player presses down the bar marked C with the left hand, and strums across the strings with the right hand. To get another chord, the player lets go of one bar, and presses down on another. You can play accompaniments to any folk song on the autoharp without reading a note of music. The accompanying chords are usually included in printed folk-song music.

You can probably learn to accompany yourself on the autoharp on your own. Perhaps you might want to read through Harry Taussig's instruction manual, *Folkstyle Autoharp*, published by Oak Publications, Inc., New York, 1967. You might also want to listen to some recordings made by the Carter Family to hear how they use the autoharp to accompany their folk singing.

The mountain dulcimer is another simple accompanying instrument for beginning folk singers. It is cheap to buy and easy to play. The magazine *Sing Out* carries ads for places to buy autoharps and dulcimers. You might even want to make your own. Here are a few books that can help: *The Mountain Dulcimer, How to Make and Play It (After a Fashion)* by Howard W.

The simplest instrument for accompanying folk singing is the autoharp. The instrument can be held either on your lap or up in the air. (Illustration by Robert Galster)

[111]

Mitchell, published in Sharon, Connecticut, Folk Legacy Records, 1965; John F. Putnam's *The Plucked Dulcimer, How To Make and Play It*, Berea, Kentucky, 1961; and Jean Ritchie's *The Dulcimer Book*, published by Oak Publications, Inc., New York, 1963.

Of all the folk instruments, however, the guitar is the most popular, and for many, the most convenient one to play. Although it is difficult to learn to play the guitar extremely well, it is quite easy to learn to play it well enough to accompany yourself.

As with the autoharp, you do not need to be able to read music to play the basic chords on the guitar. The chord names, as we said, are printed with the words of most folk songs. Or if you do not see the chord name, look for diagrams, called tablature, which are usually printed over the music. They show which fingers to press down, and where, on each string.

Below are tablatures that show you how to play many of the basic chords on the guitar. Don't attempt to learn all the chords at once. Learn the ones that you need for a song. Try playing the songs in this book with the chords that are printed over the words. You will find that the chords will become familiar as you go along.

GUITAR CHORDS

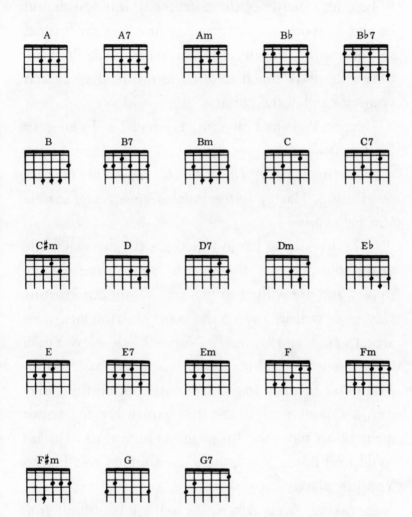

Knowing how to strum is also part of learning how to play the guitar. Again, it takes years of study to become a master of the instrument. But you should be able to work out your own strums in a short time, so you can accompany yourself. These Oak Publications titles have much information to help you teach yourself to play the guitar:

Seeger, Pete, and Silverman, Jerry, *The Folksinger's Guitar Guide*

Silverman, Jerry, *The Art of the Folk-Blues Guitar*

Taussig, Harry, *Instrumental Techniques of American Folk Guitar*

The five-string banjo is perhaps the most difficult of the common folk instruments. But if you are eager to play and are willing to work at it, you can learn to play it as well as any of the other instruments. Pete Seeger's *How To Play the Five-String Banjo*, New York, Oak Publications, Inc., 1961, is a good basic book. And don't be discouraged from attempting the banjo if you cannot read music. Just remember the comment of an old-time banjo player when asked if he could read notes: "Hell, there are no notes to a banjo. You just play it!"

Speaking of experimenting with folk music, you might want to make and use some home-made instruments.

If you enjoy singing to the accompaniment of a bass instrument, why not make a washtub bass? You'll need a large metal washtub, a broomstick, and about three yards of nylon fishing string.

Cut a notch in the broomstick, about one foot from an end. Tie one end of the nylon string very securely there. Turn the washtub over and use a small nail to punch a hole in the bottom. Now thread the loose end of the nylon string through the hole in the tub. Resting the other end of the broomstick on the rim of the upside-down washtub, adjust the stick so that the string falls straight into the hole you made in the center. Keep the broomstick in that position while someone else pulls the nylon string as tight as possible. Secure it inside the tub by tying a knot in the nylon.

To play the washtub bass, hold the broomstick on the rim of the tub with your left hand. Set your right foot on the tub and pluck the string with your right hand. If you want to raise the pitch, change the angle of the broomstick so the string becomes tighter. If you want to lower the pitch, change the broomstick so the string becomes looser. With some practice you will be able to control the pitch by changing the tightness of the string.

Creating your own instruments may not be for you. But if you are a devoted lover of folk music, you really should try to create your own folk songs. Just realize that most folk songs were written by ordinary people who did not have years of study in a music conservatory.

You can begin the way many folk singers begin, by writing new words to a folk song that you already know. Take any tune that you like, and fit your own new words to the melody.

You might also try working the other way around. Find a poem, a speech, or even a folk song that you know, and write your own melody. If you can write music, figure out the notes and write them down on some music paper. If not, work out the tune by singing it or trying it out on an instrument. Then memorize it in the fine tradition of many composers of folk songs who could not read or write music. Decide which way is best for you, and then do it that way.

"What should I write about?" is an early question you have to answer. The best advice is also the simplest. Write on subjects that have a special meaning and are important to you—how you feel about a person, place, or thing; something you read about in the newspaper; a story or joke you want to set to music. Don't worry if your subject seems ordinary. As long as it expresses honest and true feelings, it is a fitting subject for a folk song.

"Which comes first, the words or the music?" may be the next question you ask. Woody Guthrie had a good method. He started with the words. Then he tried to fit them to a folk-song melody which he knew. He kept changing the melody—and sometimes the words, too—until he got a good, natural-sounding fit between the words and music.

In your early efforts, try including a chorus of two or four lines that is repeated after every verse. The catchy words and melody of a chorus can help carry a song along.

Some more advice: Do not worry too much about the rhymes—the "June, moon, croon, spoon" sort of thing. It is not necessary to rhyme every line. If your song, for example, falls into a four-line pattern, it is enough to rhyme the second and fourth lines. Start your writing by deciding what you want to say or express; then search for the words.

When you have something that you like, sing it to yourself several times. Do you still like it? Are the accents of the music the same as the natural accents of the words when spoken? Try the song out on your friends. See what they think of it. Listen to their criticisms. Decide if you are satisfied, or not. Can you improve it? If not, throw it out and start over again.

Your first efforts may not be the best folk songs ever written. Even the folk-music greats wrote some songs that were not worth too much. But they kept on writing. They learned from their failures. Hopefully, you will too.

In a way, every song you sing, every tune you

make up, serves two purposes. It gives pleasure and enjoyment to you, and to others. And it carries forward the glorious traditions of folk music that stretch back thousands of years.

Folk Music Books and Records

Bibliography and Discography

Some books on folk music and folk-music collections:

Courlander, Harold. *Negro Folk Music.* New York: Columbia University Press, 1963.

Fisher, Miles M. *Negro Slave Songs in the United States.* New York: Citadel Press, Inc., 1969. Paper.

Greenway, John. *American Folk Songs of Protest.* Philadelphia, PA: University of Pennsylvania, 1953.

Lomax, Alan. *Penguin Book of American Folk Songs.* Baltimore, MD: Penguin Books, Inc., 1965. Paper.

Scott, John Anthony. *The Ballad of America.* New York: Bantam Books, Inc., 1966. Paper.

Bruno Nettl is one of the leading folk-music and ethnomusicology scholars of our time:

Nettl, Bruno. *Folk and Traditional Music of the Western Continents*. Englewood Cliffs, NJ: Prentice-Hall, Inc., 2nd ed., 1973.

————. *Introduction to Folk Music in the United States*. Detroit, MI: Wayne State University Press, 2nd ed., 1962. Paper.

————. *Music in Primitive Culture*. Cambridge, MA: Harvard University Press, 1956.

Instructions for making instruments, mostly percussion:

Mandell, Muriel, and Wood, Robert E. *Make Your Own Musical Instruments*. New York: Sterling Publishing Co., 1957.

Books on folk instruments and how to make and play them:

Ritchie, Jean. *The Dulcimer Book*. New York: Oak Publications, Inc., 1963. Paper.

Rizzetta, Sam. *Hammer Dulcimer: History and Playing*. Smithsonian Institution, Washington, D.C. 20560. Free.

Rizzetta, Sam. *Making a Hammer Dulcimer*. Smithsonian Institution, Washington, D.C. 20560. Free.

Seeger, Pete, and Silverman, Jerry. *The Folksinger's Guitar Guide*. New York: Oak Publications, Inc., 1962. Paper.

Taussig, Harry. *Folkstyle Autoharp*. New York: Oak Publications, Inc., 1967. Paper.

Personal books on folk music written by outstanding folk musicians:

Brand, Oscar. *The Ballad Mongers*. New York: Funk & Wagnalls, 1962.

Guthrie, Woodrow Wilson. *Bound for Glory*. New York: The New American Library, Inc., 1970. Paper reprint.

Seeger, Pete. *The Incompleat Folksinger*. New York: Simon & Schuster, Inc., 1972.

Books and record packages about folk instruments:

Mitchell, Howard. *The Hammered Dulcimer, How to Make It and Play It*. Folk Legacy Records.

Seeger, Pete. *How to Play the Five-String Banjo*. Folkways Records.

———. *The Twelve-String Guitar as Played by Leadbelly*. Folkways Records.

Wong, Kim Loy. *The Steel Drums of Kim Loy Wong*. Folkways Records.

A sampling of records by some leading folk music performers:

Baez, Joan. *The Joan Baez Ballad Book*. Vanguard Records.

Collins, Judy. *True Stories and Other Dreams*. Elektra Records.

Dylan, Bob. *Dylan*. Columbia Records.

Guthrie, Woody. *Dust Bowl Ballads*. Folkways Records.

Hardin, Tim. *Painted Head*. Columbia Records.

Leadbelly. *Rock Island Line*. Folkways Records.

Paxton, Tom. *How Come the Sun*. Reprise Records.

Ritchie, Jean. *Precious Moments*. Folkways Records.

Seeger, Pete. *Banks of Marble and Other Songs*. Folkways Records.

The Weavers. *The Weavers at Carnegie Hall*. Vanguard.

This magazine is devoted to all aspects of folk music:

Sing Out, 106 West 28 Street, New York, N.Y. 10001.

Oak publishes books on folk music and Folkways puts out folk-music records. Write for their free catalogs:

Folkways Records, 43 West 61 Street, New York, N.Y. 10023. Oak Publications, Inc., 33 West 60 Street, New York, N.Y. 10023.

Excellent lists of folk music books and records, all available without cost:

Harding, Robert S. *Bibliography on American Folk Instruments.* (1974) Smithsonian Institution, Washington, D.C. 20560.

Hickerson, Joseph C. *American Folklore: A Bibliography of Major Works.* (1975) Library of Congress, Washington, D.C. 20540.

Library of Congress, Music Division, Recorded Sound Section. Washington, D.C. 20540. *Folk Recordings.* (Revised 1974).

Index

Song Index

Index of First Lines